THE
JORDAN-DURHAM-CROCKETT
DOCUMENTARY

THE
JORDAN-DURHAM-CROCKETT
DOCUMENTARY

WE ARE THE JORDAN-DURHAM-CROCKETT'S

Avie Durham Ringwood-Wilbur

XULON PRESS

Xulon Press
2301 Lucien Way #415
Maitland, FL 32751
407.339.4217
www.xulonpress.com

Printed in the United States of America

Paperback ISBN-13: 978-1-6628-0594-3
Hard Cover ISBN-13: 978-1-6628-0595-0

DEDICATION

I would first like to dedicate this family documentary to the Holy Spirit and my parents who gave me the unction to work on bringing the families of Crocketts, Durhams and Jordans together. I would also like to thank all of my family for their participation and willingness to give the information needed for my research.

The purpose of this Documentary is to understand the importance of our family history. I believe that a family legacy is vital to leave so generations will know who the current and future family members are, as they continue the research. This will be a resource that the family can use for future genealogical research. It will be filed in the Library of Congress.

I have asked myself many times, where did our family start? Growing up we were kept at home working or in school learning. We did what we were told and no questions asked of our parents. Everyone needs to know their relatives. If we do not know them, it will cause the crossing of our own bloodline. This is why I need to know. So we can stop our blood line from intertwining with itself.

On behalf of all of my family members, thank you! I had the opportunity to talk to some family I have never spoken to before, such as Beulah, Virginia, Debra and Belinda. I humbly express my Gratitude. I am so grateful that you took the time to help me understand the dynamics of our family during my research.

I would like to also thank Linda, the obituary collector of the family and Josie for helping me keep everyone in the right family. I am so proud of my entire family, my Aunt Cash, Aunt Bish and Aunt Brooke who gave me information about the Crockett-Durham family during their younger days and my Aunt Avie Jordan-Hoskins and Otha Jordan who gave me information about the Jordans.

Thanking my childhood friend Brenda Mallory-Crockett, who came full circle from us growing up together to her marrying into the Crockett family and now my cousin. She was able to connect the dots that became an *ah ha* moment for me to verify much of the Crockett and Durham correct family history.

FOREWORD

Avie Ringwood-Wilbur, said the "Documentary for the Crockett, Durham and Jordan has value for the family." This book was researched and written in five months during the CoronaVirus Pandemic. God has blessed the writing of this book for the purpose of bringing our families together. There is strength in numbers and we have a large family.

Over the years the Crockett family have had Family Reunions to keep the families abreast with what was going on with the family and to introduce the new members.

Sarah Jordan-Durham family reunions started in 1998 with my mother Sarah telling my niece Beverly Durham-Basley to arrange it. Needless to say, she got busy with what Mama asked her to do. Beverly held the SJD family reunion with very high regards for three years. The year of 2000, Mama went to be with the Lord and in 2001 Beverly went to be with the Lord. We continue the SJD family reunion to the best of our abilities, missing Mama and Beverly every year.

The SJD Family Reunion is normally held the second weekend of August starting Friday, Saturday and Sunday. Except for 2019, the second weekend of August 10, my niece Beverly, baby daughter Trell (died). August 2020, COVID-19 pandemic cancelled the family Reunion.

In 2004 some of the families in the second generation started a Durham-Crockett and Jordan family reunion without proper notification and permission from the families involved. When we get a family reunion together that consists of the Durham-Crockett's and Jordan's, we all need to come together and let the majority rule.

I Pray that this family grow in a deeper knowledge of what Jesus Christ of Nazareth has already done. Understand, we serve a King and his kingdom, the Bible consists of Principle and Laws, we live in a world of Seed-Time and Harvest.

It is God's will that we prosper and be in health, living according to his word by faith and believing what Jesus has already done (WDJD) what did Jesus do?
"It is finished."

Regina Clay
USA Director, Durham, Crockett, Jordan Documentary

TABLE OF CONTENTS

THIS IS HOW THE FAMILIES OF JORDAN-DURHAM-CROCKETT CONNECT TOGETHER...

S arah Jordan was the oldest of the four children, she was also the first girl of the four children born to Luther and Emily Jordan.

Zefnia Durham Sr. (Zap) was the second oldest child and the oldest son of sixteen children born to Calvin and Annie Crockett-Durham.

Sarah Jordan met Zefnia Durham Sr. in 1937. They were united in marriage in 1937, she became Sarah Jordan Durham. They were married for 40 years before his death on February 4, 1977. Sarah and Zefnia Sr. gave birth to (14) fourteen children.

The first child died at birth, but she never gave up hope. Sarah and Zap as his friends called him, had thirteen more children, of which the twelve were healthy. The thirteenth child died at birth.

Now, they had twelve children for many years. In December 1966 the oldest child died of an aneurysm of the brain. Her name was Everlean Durham-Anderson (Gina), she was 28 years of age. Married to Zedward Anderson Sr., she left seven children and a husband to mourn, their baby was six months old when she died. She also left six sisters and five brothers that loved her dearly.

In 1977 Zefnia Durham (Zap) Sr. (Daddy) died, which Mom had a pretty rough time. She missed him dearly after he died. In 2000 Sarah (Mama) died, my world stopped for at least two weeks, she Loved me, I knew it. In 2009 Zefnia Durham II and Marshall Durham Sr. died (7) seven weeks aparts. There are (9) children left in the Jordan-Durham Family (6) six girls and (3) boys. Thanking God for the book Ecclesiastes, knowing there is a time for all things. It is now time for the Family to know that you are all Loved!

GRANDCHILDREN'S POEM
WE ALL HAD A PLACE IN HER HEART

There was an old lady who lived in a shoe. She had so many children, she didn't know what to do. She sat on the porch and scratched her head, fed them some grits and put them to bed. This was good everyone may say. But I have a better one that goes this way. There once was an old lady who lived in Spring Valley, she had seven girls; One we called Sally (Sarah), Martha, Avie, Annie, Emily (Siccy), Josephine, and sweet Everlean. Now I'll say that's truly a bunch, but she had (5) boys to make some lunch.

Their names are Marshall, Morgan, James and Zef and let's not forget John he can't be left out. Now this house is full and you agree, with a head shake but Everlean passed on, so 7 grandchildren were in need of a home. Your eyes grow wide and you say, "No Way" but no one asked you. I hear her say, as she goes about her merry way. Now she was not alone for Zap was there to lend a hand and do his Part: but most was on Grandma for she had a big Heart.

Now, there was room in Grandmother's heart for everyone. If it was a boy he was treated like a son. She did all she could and others would get mad, because that person was sent home for being so bad. Grandma showed Love despite what she faced, in her heart, where we all found a place. Whether you were dark, light, short, tall, thin or fat, she loved all of us unselfishly until her death. She fought for three days so we all could rest.

Jesus said that in my father's house there are many rooms, that he was going to prepare for us. Grandma prepared a place for everyone in her heart, We will always Love you Grandma and miss you.

By: Zefnia Durham III

THE CROCKETT-DURHAM'S
WITH SISTERS AND BROTHERS AND THEIR CHILDREN

Annie Crockett who had 2 Sisters (Carrie Crockett-Height, Betty Crockett-Ford) and she also had (6) brothers. Coleman Crockett, Marshall Crockett, Tom Crockett, Aaron Sampson Crockett, Malachi and Heavy Crockett (Twins).

Aaron Sampson Crockett Sr. married Idle B. Day-Crockett, **They had 13 Children.**
Their children: Enoch Crockett (Dean), Aaron Sampson Crockett II, Beulah Crockett-Floyd, Virginia Crockett-Carswell, Lola Crockett-Stephens, Nancy Crockett-Wilmore, Mae Ola Crockett-McBryer, Willie Pank Crockett-Flowers, Lillie Bell Crockett-Anderson, Roberta Crockett-Wilmore, Shedrick Crockett, Nemiah Crockett and Paul Crockett.
Their Children:
Enoch Crockett Sr. (Dean) (Died 2020), married Hazel L. Crockett, **Their children:**
Jimmy Crockett, married Linda Crockett, Elizabeth C. Dunlap, Enoch Crockett Jr., Evelyn D. Crockett, Joan Crockett married Harry Shine, Andrew Crockett and Jacquline M. William. Enoch and Hazel had (12) Grandchildren , (3) Great grandchildren.

Their Children:
Aaron Sampson Crockett Jr. (died 2005) married Sallie Kate Hill-Crocket (2019)
Their Children: Aaron Sampson Crockett III, Jerry Crockett, Ronnie Crockett, Eric Crockett (Snicker), Ethel Crockett (Phine) and Brenda Crockett.

Aaron Sampson Crockett III, married Rosemerry Crockett. **Their children:** Corey Stephens-Crockett, Shuneca Crockett and Dedrick Crockett.
Their children: Shuneca Crockett-Gundy married,
Her children: Brooke Gundy and Tyler Gundy.

Dedrick Crockett married, with Children.

Jerry Crockett married Cheryl Crockett, **Their Children:** Andrea Crockett, Veronica Crockett, Jessica Crockett and One Son.

Ronnie Crockett married Brenda Mallory-Crockett, **Their Children:** Ariane B. Crockett and Wonchina U. Williams.
Ariane B. Crockett, Her Child: Amina Channin Veal.

Eric Crockett (Snicker), (died) married with Children.

Ethel Crockett (Phinne), She has (1) Child

Brenda Crockett, She has (2) Children

Beulah Crockett-Floyd married Prince J. Floyd Sr., (Died) 2009.
Their Children: Belinda R. Floyd and Prince J. Floyd Jr.

Virginia Crockett-Carswell married Arthur Carswell Sr., **Their Children:**
Debra Crockett-Carswell, Arthur L. Carswell Jr., Milton Carswell and Willie J. Carswell.
Debra Crockett-Taylor married Collar Taylor.

Lola Crockett-Stephens, married, She has 4 children and her husband died.

Nancy Crockett-Wilmore, married She has one Child.

Willie Pank Crockett-Flowers, married, with Children, her husband died.

Mae Ola Crockett-McBryer died, she married with Children.

Lillie Bell Crockett-Anderson died, she married with Children.

Roberta Crockett-Long died, married with Children.

Shedrick Crockett died, married with Children.

Nemiah Crockett died, married with Children.

Paul Crockett died, married with Children

Sarah Jordan, born September 19, 1921 to the parents of **Emily Stephens-Jordan, 1902-1983 and Luther Jordan Sr. 1900-1982**

Luther Jordan Sr. His mother's name is Lula Jordan and his father's name is Tillman Jordan. Three sisters: Rosa Jordan Dodson, Leila Jordan-Lewis (Aunt Jabe),
And Classic Jordan-Wimberly, and two brothers Norman Jordan and Mack Jordan.

Rosa Jordan Dodson**, Her Children:** Daisy Lee Harris and Lucy M. Farris

Daisy Lee Harris, **Her children:** Ethel Harris (Sister) and James Harris (Died), married and had 3 girls and one boy (died).

Emily Stephens-Jordan, Her mother, Hattie Fault-Stephens and her Father's name Lemon Stephens. She had (1) one sister Marie Stephens-Gainey.
Her Child: Hazel Gainey, **Her Child:** Wayne Gainey,

THE JORDAN FAMILY AND THEIR CHILDREN

Sarah Jordan-Durham born September 19, 1921-September 4, 2000 to the parents of **Emily Jordan-1902-1983 and Luther Jordan Sr. 1900-1982** who gave birth to **four children:** Sarah Jordan, James Jordan, Luther Jordan Jr. and Josephine Jordan Sarah Jordan was the oldest of the four children.

Their Children:

James Jordan married Avie L. Jordan-Hoskins
His Children: Lottie Jordan-Harvin, Robert Jordan Sr. (died), Stanley Jordan,
and Jennifer Jordan.
Lottie Jordan-Harvin, married Harold Harvin Sr.
Their children: Harold Harvin Jr. and Natalie Harvin.
Natalie Harvin, Her Child: Donta Jordan-Harvin: Her son has (2) Two Children.
Robert Jordan Sr. (died 1986), married Irene Robertson-Jordan.
Their children: Karin Jordan, Katrina Jordan and Robert Jordan Jr.

Luther Jordan Jr. (Uncle Little Buddy), married Dorothy Kay and Divorced,died.
His Son: Otha Jordan
His Children: Kenyatta Jordan, Alex Jordan, Tarkitta Jordan.
Their Children:
Kenyatta Jordan, Her children: Jassaray Jordan, Nadia James-Jordan, Nicholas Roby-Jordan, and Noah Roby-Jordan.
Tarkitta Jordan, Her Child: Amonei Jordan-Mathis
Alex Jordan, His Child: Shanylah Jordan

Josephine Jordan-Mallory- married Charles Mallory
Her Son: Johnny B. Jordan (Killer Red) married Lois Simeton-Jordan
Their Children: Hansel Jordan, Jonathan Jordan and Chaka Jordan
Chaka Jordan, Her children: Mckayla Jordan-Hollings, Saveryiana Jordan-Hollings and Jaiden Pegram.

THE JORDAN-DURHAM'S

Sarah Jordan met Zefnia Durham Sr. in 1937. They were united in marriage in June 1937. She is now **Sarah Jordan Durham.** Sarah gave birth to **fourteen children.**

Their Children:

1. Emma Lee Durham — — died at birth
2. Everlean Durham Anderson — - June 25,1939 died 12-1966
3. Martha L. Durham-Glawson — -March 19,1941
4. Zefnia Durham Jr — -January 1,1944 died 2009
5. James Durham — -November 27,1945
6. Emily Durham — -October 7,1946
7. Annie Durham — -December 3,1948
8. Marshall Durham Sr. — -October 10,1950 died-2009
9. Sarah L. Durham-Nelson — -October 16,1952
10. Morgan L. Durham — -December 15,1954
11. John Durham — -September 29,1956
12. Avie L. Durham-Wilbur — -October 5,1958
13. Norma L. Durham — -died at birth
14. Josephine Durham-Chapman — -June 21,1961

1. Emma L. Durham —Died at Birth

2. Everlean Durham-Anderson, June 25, 1939-1966 married to Zedward Anderson Sr.

Their children: Joey Anderson Sr, Martha A. Anderson-Stephens, Marilynette Anderson-Thomas, Connie Anderson, Zedward Anderson Jr., Harriet Anderson and Lisa Anderson.

Joey Anderson Sr. born 1956—2018 married to Lola Hollingsworth-Anderson
His children: Joey Anderson Sr. has (30) Grandchildren, according to his oldest daughter Guiesel L. Anderson-Wilson.
Guiesel L. Anderson Wilson, Latoya Robinson-Anderson, Lazedra Anderson Khari K. Hollingsworth-Anderson, Deomeseo Stephens-Anderson, Marquis Jackson-Anderson, Pearl Thomas-Anderson, Amarah Carson-Anderson, Joey Anderson Jr. and Alaye Carson-Anderson.
Their Children:
Guiesel L. Anderson-Wilson, Her Children: Akevia Wilburn (Josephine), George Wilson, Jemremiah Wilson, Marquez Veal and Assyria Wilson.
Akevia Wilburn (Josephine), Her Children: Kingston Wilburn and Kari Wilburn.

Latoya Robinson-Anderson, Her Child: Nekotisha Robinson, Norrazious Young (Taman).

Khari K. Hollingsworth-Anderson, married, **His children:** Kyreeion Butler

Deomeseo Stephens-Anderson (Deo), His Children: Ojavi Stephens and Demontrez Stephens.

Marquis Jackson-Anderson, His Children: Jordan Jackson, Khyell Jackson, Omaria Jackson, Ari Jackson, and Jackson.

Lazedra Anderson (Queen), she has 4 Children one of **Her Children:**
Ma'liyah Anderson.

Martha A. Anderson-Stephens-married Kenneth Stephens.
Her children: Federial Anderson and Aisha Anderson
Aisha Anderson-Elvine-married Ulysess Elvine (Redman).
Their Children: Jalen Anderson-Wimberly and Juwam Anderson-Wimberly (Twins), Destiny Anderson-Wimberly , Shaquan Anderson-Elvine, La'Vourea Anderson-Elvine, Da'Vourea Anderson-Elvine (Twins) and Damarquez Anderson-Elvine
Their Children: Jalen Anderson-Wimberly-His children: Orlando Wimberly and Brooklyn Wimberly.
Federial Anderson
Her Children: Zekia Anderson, Jamarion Anderson-Stephens, and Jazeon Anderson-Stephens.
Their Children:
Zekia Anderson-Madelyn Anderson

Marilynette Anderson-Stephens-Thomas, married to Norman Thomas. (D) E. Stephens.
Their children: LeArneca V. Anderson-Stephens and Lynnyonna V. Anderson-Stephens.
LeArneca V. Anderson-Middleton married Mikal Middleton.
Their Children: Shaniyah D. Anderson, Mikiyah A. Middleton and MiLayah C. Middleton.
Lynnyonna V. Anderson-Berry, married Dominic Berry.
Their Children: Quadre Anderson-Stephens, married Alondra Stephens,
Their Children: Caleb Anderson-Stephens and Lucas J. Anderson-Stephens.

Connie Anderson—Boisy Wilson Jr. died 2011.
Their Children: Kia V. Anderson, Taria L. Anderson-White, and Donta K. Anderson.
Their children:
Taria L. Anderson-White married Jarvis White
Akedria J. Anderson, Ahniquah P. Wilmore, Auteria Y. Wilmore and Jiden White.
Akedria J. Anderson- Acelynn N. Glover
Ahniquah P. Wilmore- Ava M. Wilmore
Kia V. Anderson-Her children: De'Avion S. Albritton, Na'Tijalyn A. Albritton.
Donta K. Anderson, His children: Temaya N. Ballard-Anderson, Kayla Ballard-Anderson and Royal A. Anderson.

Zedward Anderson Jr., His Children: Sharod Watkins-Anderson Malik Moore-Anderson and Zaedan Anderson.
Their Children:
Sharod J. Watkins-Anderson Sr, His Children: Tykirra Watkins-Anderson,
Shariyah Watkins-Anderson, Sharod Watkins-Anderson Jr.
Shamarion Watkins-Anderson, Shytirra Watkins-Anderson, Asia Watkins-Anderson,
and Kash Watkins-Anderson

Harriet Anderson: Her Children: Theakos Lamar Anderson, LaTisha T Anderson, James Linel Anderson Sr., Tajai Dupree Hicks-Anderson
Their Children:
Theakos Lamar Anderson, His Children: Isaiah Ny'Mir Butler and I'Zeriah Lamy Anderson.
LaTisha T Anderson, her children: Genesis Anderson
James Linel Anderson Sr., married to Deborah Kasandra Anderson James Linel Anderson Jr., Jayden Gregory Anderson, Jamiyah Elisa Anderson and
Joshua Lee Anderson.
Tajai Dupree Hicks-Anderson, His Children: James Linel Anderson Zakai Vincent Hicks-Anderson.

Lisa Anderson, Her Children: Tedriono Anderson (Ted), Chachi D. Anderson and Chitara Yasmine Anderson.
Tedriono Anderson, Has (3) Children.

Chachi Anderson married, ShaTara Grant-Anderson,
Their Children: Kacin Grant Anderson, Dekevion Anderson, Kamryn Grant-Anderson, Dasani Anderson, Nyaissa Anderson, Lefania Anderson, Journie Anderson, Kadyn Grant-Anderson, Zoe Anderson, Koby Anderson, Kirsten Anderson,
Jacion Anderson, Gabriel Anderson, Abigail Anderson, Victoria Grant-Anderson, Kristen Scott-Anderson.

Chitara Yasmine Anderson (Yas):
Her daughter; Takyla A. Anderson-Turner.

3. Martha L. Durham-Glawson born March 19,1941 married to Richard B. Glawson Sr. born December 8,1941-May 29,2011, **Their Child: Linda Durham-Thorpe born July 28,1959** married Leroy Thorpe Jr. (died 2009), **Their Child:** Tamara M. Thorpe-Foster married Gregory J. Foster.
Their Children: Brandon J. Foster, Makayla D. Foster and (Baby).

4. Zefnia Durham Jr., born January 1, 1944-2009, married to Hattie Mae William-Durham born July 20, 1944-2011
Their Children:
Selina Gail William-Dyches, Andrea L. Durham-Collier, Keturia R. Durham-Cooper-Weaver, Zefnia Durham III and Zeward Durham.

Selina Gail William-Dyches married to Stanley Dyches Sr.
Their children: Stanley Dyches Jr. and Christrain Celino Dyches

Andrea L. Durham—Collier married to Tommy Collier
Her children: Tiffany M. Durham, Andrew R. Durham Sr., and Christopher E. Durham
Their Children:
Tiffany M. Durham- **Her child:** Ava Durham-Carter
Andrew R. Durham-**His child:** Andrew R. Durham Jr. (AJ)

Christopher E. Durham-**His children:** Leah Durham and Carmen Durham

Keturia R. Durham-Cooper-Weaver married to Vincent Weaver **Their children:** Kamesha M. McCray, Courtney W. Cooper and Coreon Cooper.
Zefnia Durham III Divorced-1988/Married to Wanda Durham.
His children: Selena C. Durham/died—, Zefnia Durham IV, Shayna C. Durham, Zephaniah L. Durham.
Zefnia Durham IV, **His children:**—Zaniah L. Durham, Zefnia Durham V (Z5), Zakhar Durham.

Zeward Durham/ No children

5. James Durham born November 27, 1945 married Lenora Culverton-Durham (Died)
His children: Subrina Parker-Brown, Tameka Durham-Parker, Lamar Durham-Parker, and Chad Durham-Scott.
Their Children:
Subrina Parker-Durham-Brown, Vincent (vinny) Brown, Madelius (deli), Menishia (nisha), Rodricus (drick) Vintambria (montmont) Parker Brown
Their Children: Cardashia, Jamarion, Malaysia

Tameka Durham-Parker, Her son: Kenan Parker-Baker
His Children: Chandler Parker-Baker

Lamar Durham-Parker, His son: Isaiah Parker-Durham

Chad Scott-Durham-His Children: Korin Scott-Durham, Kie Scott-Durham, Chaden Scott-Durham, Chad Scott-Durham Jr.
Their Children: Korin Scott-Durham. **Her Children:** Khloe Scott-Durham and Chase Scott-Durham. Kie Scott-Durham. **Her Child:** Kenna Scott-Durham.

6. Emily Durham-Wilson, born October 7, 1946, Frank Harris died 12-1995 later married to Boisy Wilson.

Her Children: Jo Ann Durham-Glover-Height and Beverly Y. Durham- Basley August 10,1965-August 2001 and Nytavious J. Veal. **Also, Raising:** Trinity Yvonne Coley Great-granddaughter.
Their Children:
Jo Ann Durham-Glover-Height (Divorced) & married to Samuel Height.
Their children: Yakcreona Glover, Aja Glover and Samuel Terrell Height,
Their children:
Aja Minyun Glover—Her Child: Ja'Niyah Ann Glover
Yakcreona Marie Glover—N/C
Samuel Terrell Height——Samuel Terrell Height, Jr. and Samaya Jo'Leah Height

Beverly Y. Durham-Basley August 10,1965- August 2001, married Oscar Basley Jr.
Their Children: Ariel J. Basley and Shaneka Antrell Basley
Ariel J. Basley- Her Child: Duane Deontaye Patterson
Shaneka Antrell Basley-2- 7-1987 to 8-10-2019,
Her daughter: Trinity Yvonne Coley.

7. Annie Durham-Raven born December 3, 1948 married Wendell Raven,
Their Daughter: Treshetta Raven-Sims married to Stefan Sims Sr.,
Their children: Stefan Sims Jr. and Selah Sims.

8. Marshall Durham Sr. born October 10,1950-September 3, 2009. **His children:** Marshall Durham Jr., Cindy Durham-Curry, Tracy Durham and Crystal Durham-Stephens
Their children:
Marshall Durham Jr., married with Children.
Cindy Durham Curry, married Dexter Curry, They have Children.
Tracy Durham, Has (2) children.
Crystal Durham-Stephens, married Trawick Stephens Sr.,
Their Children:
Quenasha Stephens, Chantrell Stephens, Trawick Stephens Jr. and Christain Stephens.

9. Sarah L. Durham-Wilson-Nelson born 10-16-1952 married to Eugene Nelson Sr.
Eugene Durham-Nelson Jr. No children. (Died 4-2020).

Demetrius Durham-Wilson, married to Shantell Wilson.
His children: Deanerius Dontey Wilson, Machai Johnson-Wilson, Solomon Johnson-Wilson, Journey Johnson-Wilson and Demetria McClallum-Wilson.
Their children:
Deanerius Dontey Wilson
His Children: Dontey J. Wilson and Kaydence E. Wilson

10. Morgan L. Durham -12- 15-1954 married to
Mona Johnson-Durham.
His Children: Corey Harris-Durham, Kelly Harris-Durham, Ali Harris-Durham, TaNeatua Mokina Harris-Durham (Boo Boo) died 2013, Nakeeba (KeKe) Johnson-Durham and Maureen Wilder-Durham
Their Children:
Corey Harris-Durham-His daughter-TaniNylah Anderson-Durham

Kelly Harris-Durham married Lydia Wilkes-Harris
Their Children: Katorah Harris, Timothy Engram-Harris (PeeWee) and Kelly Isley Harris (Little Kelly) Katorah Durham-Harris. **Her Children:** Ke'moure Banks, Khylee Banks & Kentley Speed (2020 baby).

TaNeatua Mokina Harris-Durham (Boo Boo) 1976-2013.
Her son: Noah M. Harris

Ali L. Harris-Durham (Var),
His Children: Alianna Strazzeri-Harris and
(Raising) Noah M. Harris, his nephew.

Devar Burke-Durham (BJ), has (1) Child

11. John Durham 9-29-1956 married Annie Bell Emory-Durham
Their Child: Shameraye Durham
Her children: Jada Durham, and Ah'Nylah Durham (Bug).

12. Avie Durham Ringwood-Wilbur born 10-05-1958, married James E. Ringwood died-1980 married to Arthur Will-Wilbur
Their sons, Tellas D. Durham-Ringwood Sr., and Michael Wilbur.
Tellas D. Durham-Ringwood Sr. and Troylicia Robertson-Ringwood,
Their Children:
Tylah D. Ringwood, Tayden D. Ringwood and Tellas D. Ringwood Jr.
Michael Wilbur: His Children: Zachary Wilbur and Caroline Wilbur.
God Grandchildren: Dhimon Hines, Deante Hines, Dasia Hines & Davion Hines.
Their Children:
Dhimon Hines-Her Child: Brenden Scantler and 2021 baby.
Deante Hines-married Lisa Maldonado-Hines, **Their Child:** Angeliz Hines

13. Norma L. Durham—-died at birth

14. Josephine Durham-Chapman born June 21,1961 married Ronald Chapman.
Their children: Brandy Shunti Chapman and Tysean Kotta Chapman.
Brandy S. Chapman-Farrow-Ex-Husband-Willie Farrow Jr.
Their children: Nakira Farrow, Nykeem Farrow and Nykeze Farrow
Tysean K. Durham-Chapman married Renee Pace-Chapman, **Their children:** Aniyah Jackson-Chapman, Tyvareah Chapman.

THE CROCKETT-DURHAM'S

Annie Crockett, and Calvin Durham Sr.
who gave birth to sixteen (16) children.
We could not account for but, Thirteen (13) children.

Their Children:
Zefnia Durham Sr. and Vestie Durham who died at birth, his Twin
Sister, Bobby Link Durham Sr, Lorene Durham (Aunt Brooke),
Lisa Mae Durham (died at birth) Ollie Mae Durham,
Kathleen Durham-Blackshear (Aunt Cash),
Elosie Durham-Tharpe (Aunt Bish) Twin Sisters,
Louise Durham-Hughes (Aunt Lish),
Calvin Durham Jr., Pauline Durham-Curtis,
Christine Durham-Hill Martha L. Durham-Fitzpatrick.
Ollie Mae Durham-Rouse-married to Joseph Rouse.
Her Children:
Mark Henry Durham, Willie Durham (Doc), Arthur L. Rouse/His
twin brother died at birth.
Their Children: Willie T. Durham (Doc), married Tilda Durham.
Their Child: Mary A. Durham.
Mary Ann Durham, **Her Child:** Arrika Durham

Arthur L. Durham-Rouse died (2014) married Ruby Rouse.
Their Children:
Valerie Rouse-Gray married Melvin Gray Jr., **Their Children:**
Tai'ramone Rouse-Gray, Denario Rouse-Gray, Asha Rouse-Gray,
Akil Gray, Nailah Gray, and Talibah Gray.

Mark Henry Durham-Rouse Sr. died (2017) married
Alberta S. Rouse.
Their Children: Linda Rouse-Green, Mark H. Durham-Rouse Jr.,
Allie Rouse and Rose M. Rouse.

Zefnia Durham Sr. born October 7, 1919 died February 4, 1977 married **Sarah Durham** they had 14 children (2) died at birth.

Kathleen Durham-Blackshear (Aunt Cash) 1925-2020 married Mckinley Blackshear,
Their Child: Sarah J. Durham-Denson (Miamai) (2017)
Her children: Shirley B. Anthony-Slay, Jacqueline Blackshear-Anthony and Jasper Blackshear (BroBro)

Their Children:
Shirley Blackshear-Anthony-Slay married Earl Slay: **Their children:** Roger D. Anthony Jr., Travis Anthony, Terrell Anthony and Tamaras Anthony.
Their Children:
Roger D. Anthony Jr. (Died 2019). Married Shakette Anthony.
Their Daughter: London R. Anthony
Travis Anthony married Tayna Anthony (died) 2015/No children.
Terrell Anthony married Erica Anthony (Divorce) **Their Children:** Nykala Anthony.
Tamaras Anthony, married Ciara Mack-Anthony,
Their children: Corey Mack-Anthony and Tamarcus Anthony (Birth 2020)

Jacqueline Howard-Anthony, married John Anthony.
Their Children: Makrisha LaShern Howard (died-2017), Antonzio Anthony, Govannio Anthony and Christopher Anthony.
Their Children:
Makrisha LaShern Howard (Died 2017), **Her Children:** Donnie Howard and Tamesha Howard.
Their Children:
Tamesha Howard-Brown, married Michal Brown Sr., **Their Children:** Ayden Howard, Noah Brown,Timothy Brown, Kinsely Brown and Michal Brown Jr.
Antonzio Anthony, married Nakesha W. Anthony. **His Children:** Ariel Anthony and Toniah Anthony.
Govannio Anthony, His Children: Destiny Pitts-Anthony.

Christopher Anthony Sr., His Children: Christopher Anthony Jr., Tychristalynn Anthony, Christyle Anthony, Christianna Meadow-Anthony, Govannio Anthony, Maya Durham-Anthony, Deshawn Anthony.

Jasper Blackshear (brobro) married Tara Jones-Blackshear **His Children:** Quisha Blackshear, Jermaine Blackshear.
Jermaine Blackshear, His Children: Kenori L. Wilkerson-Blackshear, Jerliya A. Jenkins-Blackshear, Ja'mesiya Z. Wilmore-Blackshear and Jermaine G. Blackshear.

Elosie Durham-Tharpe (Aunt Bish) married Jerry Tharpe, **Their children:** Martha N. Tharpe-Basley, Emma Jean Tharpe and Thomas Tharpe Sr. (Peeba) 1950-2018.

Their children:
Martha N. Tharpe-Basley-Her Children: Kenneth Tharpe (died 2012) Nicole Tharpe, Edith Tharpe and Everett Tharpe (Twins).
Their Children:
Kenneth Tharpe Sr. (died 2012), **His Children:** Delisha Tharpe, Johnathan Tharpe and Kenneth Tharpe Jr.
Nicole Tharpe-Glover-Ingram, Divorced.
Their Children: JaQue Shonquez Glover Sr., Chelsea K. Hall and Carl A. Ingram Jr.
Their Children:
JaQue Shonquez Glover, married Shernell Farrow-Tharpe.
Their Children:
JaQue Shonquez Glover Jr., Jasmeria Tharpe-Hart and Kinsley Nicole Tharpe-Glover.
Edith Tharpe-Mallory-Hart, Divorced.
Their Children: Demonte' Tharpe-Mallory, Chasma Tharpe-Hart, and Ron Tharpe-Hart.
Their Children:
Demonte' Tharpe-Mallory married Jessika Mallory. **Their Child:** A'nia Brielle Mallory.
Everrett Tharpe married Juanita Tharpe, **Their Children:** Makalyla Tharpe and Brandon Tharpe.

Thomas Tharpe Sr. (Peeba, died 2018)
His children: Lesley Cobb-Tharpe, Tammy Veal-Tharpe, Patrick Cobb-Tharpe, Toby Veal-Tharpe, Damious Ford-Tharpe, Hector Love-Tharpe, Thomas Tharpe Jr.
Their Children:

Emma Jean Tharpe— Her Children: Charles Tharpe, Jason Tharpe, Marquetta Tharpe, Veronica Tharpe.
Their Children:
Charles Tharpe-His children: Charles Tharpe III, Caleah Tharpe
Jason Tharpe- His Children: Jada Tharpe, Jason Tharpe Jr.,
Marquetta Tharpe- married Robert Thomas. **Their children:** Sacajawea Tharpe-King Shakedra Tharpe, Shantia Tharpe-Thomas, Robert Tharpe-Thomas.
Their Children:
Sacajewea Tharpe-King married Christopher King,
Their children: Camaria King, Braden King and Kallin King, Christain King (died at birth) and Shakedra Tharpe.
Shakedra Tharpe-Jenkins, Her children: Xavier Jenkins, Xizola Jenkins.
Veronica Tharpe-Lott, married Clarence Lott,
Their Children; Daquavious Tharpe-Davis, Quadashia Tharpe-Lott, Enyiah Tharpe-Lott, Ashanti Tharpe (TT), Clarissa Tharpe-Lott, Angela Tharpe-Lott.
Their children:
Daquavious Tharpe-Davis married Reshunda Davis: **Their Children**, Jalen Davis, Taylor Davis, Tristan Davis.
Quadashia Tharpe-Lott- Her child: Ivey White,
Clarissa Tharpe-Lott- Her child: Kalee Lott

Louise Durham-Hughes (Aunt Lish) married William Hughes Sr.
Their Children: Charlie Lee Durham (Scooney),
Johnny Durham-Kay (Baybay)
Willie Pauline Durham-Hughes (Died),
William Durham-Hughes Jr. (Little Man),
Gloria Durham-Hughes and Mary Durham-Hughes.

Their Children:
Charlie Lee Durham-Collins (Scooney) (Died)
married Lucille Watkins-Collins.
Their Child: Subrenia Durham-Collins.(Deceased) Has children

Johnny Kay Sr. (Bebe) married **Their child:** Johnny F. Kay, Jr.,
Adrina Michelle Kay, and Dwayne Lavar Kay.
Their Children:
Johnny F. Kay, Jr., **His children:** Lavonia Kay and Isaiah Kay
Dwayne Lavar Kay. **His child:** Adonis Kay

Gloria Hughes, Her children: Antonio Young, Angela Young
(Died), Lamont Stribling, Cecil Wayne Stribling, Michael Hughes,
Sue Ann Anderson, Joseph Anderson and Tyrone Anderson.
Their Children: Lamont Stribling Sr., His children: Lamont
Stribling Jr., Kenorio Stribling
Michael Hughes, His children: Michael Hughes Jr.,
Yolanda Hughes and Keshun Hughes

Calvin Durham Jr. (Uncle Sunset) married, They had three sons;
Two sons died and **Sylvester Durham.**

Lorene Durham (Aunt Brooke),
Her Children: Larry Durham-Butler (Died 1991)
Doris Durham-Butler (Nag).
Their Children:
Doris Durham-Butler-Teresa Durham-Johnson,
Shawonda Durham-Stephens, Sheree Durham-Mays
and Emanual Durham-Burney
Their Children:
Shawonda Durham-Stephens (Boki) married Cuveas Stephens
Their Children: Ebony Durham-Brown, Endia Durham-Glover
and Noa Durham-Stephens.
Sheree Durham-Mays (BB) married Eric Mays. **Their Children:**
Eric Durham, Erion Mays and Ethan Mays.
Eric Durham, His Child: Aiden Glover

Emanual Durham-Burney, married Chelsea Burney.

Pauline Durham-Curtis (died 2018) married **Iverson Curtis (Uncle Son)** (They had no Children)

Christine Durham-Hill (died 2005) married to Albert Hill (died) **Their Children:** Ollie M. Hill (Yank), Charity M. Hill, Julia M. Hill-Harvell (Boom), Lillie M. Hill, Katie M. Hill-William (CuCu), L.B. Hill and Jackson Hill (Booster).

Ollie Mae Hill-Stephens (Yank) married
Arthur Stephens Sr. (Booty)
Their Children: Branda Hill-Stephens (Tee),
Pinky Stephens-Carswell, Arthur Hill-Stephens Jr. (Slot),
Johnny Hill-Stephens, and Chuckie Hill-Stephens
Their Children:

Branda Hill-Stephens (Tee), Her Children: Darnell Stephens, Nina Stephens and LaJohn Stephens. **Darnell Stephen Sr. His Children:** Darnell Stephens Jr. and Devin Stephens

Lucinda Hill-Stephens-Churchwell, (Died 2005), Her children: Derrick Stephens and Darnecia Stephens-Hill.

Pinky Hill-Stephens-Carswell, married Dexter Carswell. **Their Children:**
Dexter L. Carswell, Marco L. Carswell, Renata L. Carswell and **(Raising)** Derrick Stephens.
Their children:
Dexter L. Carswell, married Arnetra Carswell, **Their children:** LaJuan Carswell, Jalen Carswell and Kanye Carswell.
Marco L. Carswell, **His Children:** Markal Carswell, Marquis Carswell and Marliyah Carswell.
Renata L. Carswell, **Her Children:** Ghorain Carswell and Genesis Carswell. Derrick Stephens, **His Child:** London Mitchell-Stephens.

Johnny Hill-Stephen (Bubble), No Children.

Thanks to all who served in the Military
There are many who served, who are not Posted.

Chuckie Hill-Stephen, married Crystal Stephens. They have Children.

Arthur Hill-Stephen Jr. (Slot), married Debra Stephens. They have Children.

Joseph Hill-Stephen (Mitchell), No Children.

Dale Hill-Stephen (Pop), (Died), He has (2) Two Children

Everlyn Hill-Stephen, (Died).

Charity M. Hill-Butler (9-2020), Emmitt Butler (Sonny) (died 2020).
Their Children:
Freddy Hill-Jones (Sugar boy), Marie Hill-Butler, Emmitt Hill-Butler Jr., Brenda Hill-Ford, Calloway Hill-Butler, Earl Hill-Butler, Ulysses Hill-Butler (Polon), Kenneth Hill-Butler, Ronnie Hill-Butler, Richard Hill-Butler and Queenester Hill-Robertson died (2020).

Freddy Hill-Jones (Sugar boy, died 2000), married Betty Jones (died 2011).
Their Children: Freddie Jones Jr., Scherell Jones and Scherri Jones.
Freddie Jones Jr.,married Shemeka Jones. **Their Children:** Jalexxus Jones, Britney Jones, Zion Jones, Ciara Jones, Freddrika Jones, Dayjja Jones, Tyree Jones, Kaiden Jones, and Kaidence Jones.
Their Children:
Jalexxus Jones, Her Children: Trayvion Holvendorf, Joryyahia Worthy and Josiah Worth.
Scherell Jones, married Alonzo Jenkins. **Their Children:** Dani Jones, Schyniah Jenkins, Jalen Jenkins and Kiara Jenkins
Dani Jones, Her Child: Christian Jones.
Scherri Jones, Her Child: Kamiyah James

Marie Butler (Spank), Her Children: To'shiko Butler, Nayona Butler (Kim)
Their Children: To'shiko Butler, Her children: Kyreeion Butler and Jadayvion Butler.
Nayona Butler (Kim), Her children: Se'quioa Butler, Kamauree Butler and Charity M. Butler-Paschal.

Emmitt Butler Jr. (Mama), married Sharon Butler, They have (3) Children.

Ulysses Butler Sr. (Polon), **His Children:** Ulysses Butler Jr., and Ashely Butler.

Earl Butler, Has (5) Children.

Brenda Butler-Ford married David Ford. **Their children:** Cedrick Arnett Butler Vonrico La'Deuntae Ford and Kieona La'Vesia Ford.
Their children:
Cedrick Arnett Butler, His children: Tyara Elizabeth Butler, Dyneccia T. Butler, Cedrick Arnett Butler Jr., Ced L. E. Butler, Emanyuel D. Butler, Marquez T. Butler and Cedrion T. Butler.
Vonrico La'Deuntae Ford, Her Child: Jae'l Jefferson
Kieona La'Vesia Ford, Her child: Raekwonna Brenyara Kieshawonnna Ford.
Their children:
Raekwonna Brenyara Kieshawonnna Ford, Her child: Jayla Amoura Burroughs
Dyneccia T. Butler, Her children: Miangel Taylor and Elijah Ross.

Kenneth Butler, married Vicky Butler, they have (4) Children.

Ronnie Butler, has (3) Children. Creccia Butler, Chachi Butler and Kelly Butler (Died 2013).
Richard Butler (Man), has children.

Queenester Hill-Robertson died (7-2020), married Rodney Robinson. **Their children:**
Franklin Harvey, Breadle Wilcox, Rodney Robinson III and Joseph Robinson.
Their children: Joseph Robinson Jr., Viceson Harrell, Aasiyah Q. Wilcox, Armani Robinson.

Julia M. Hill-Harvey (Boom) married Tommie Harvey
Their Children: Cynthia Hill-Wimberly,
and Cornell Hill-Sylvester (Tony).
Their Children:
Cynthia Hill-Dixion married Benjamin Heard,
Her son: Aaron Dixion-Heard
Cornell Hill-Sylvester (Tony) married Veronica J. Sylvester.
Their Children: Tiven Sylvester, Terrell Sylvester
and Messiah Sylvester. (Tony, has 2 sets of Twins).

Lillie M. Hill- (died), Her Child: Willie Mae Hill (Bean)
Willie Mae Hill (Bean), Her Children: Shatorya Hill-Blackshear,
Jerome Hill, Latela Hill-Anderson.
Their Children:
Shatorya Hill-Blackshear married Torrence Blackshear.
Their Child: Tekebrion Blackshear
Jerome Hill, His Children: Trinity Lewis-Hill, Jerome Hill Jr.
Latela Hill-Anderson married Derrick Harris-Harvell.
Their Children: Taria Hill-Harvell, Trent Hill-Harvell and
Takobe Hill-Harvell.

Katie M. Hill-William (Cucu), married Billy William.
Their Children: Caroline Scott (Bet), and Michael Hill.

L.B. Hill married Shirlene Hill, **Their Children:**
They have Children and (Raising) Darnecia Stephens-Hill,

Jackson Hill (Booster) married Mary Ola William-Hill.
Their Children: Lonnie J.William-Hill (Pee wee) and
Calvin L. William-Hill and John Albert Hill.

Lonnie J. William-Hill (Pee wee), His Children:
Lonnie J. William-Crouch Jr., Carl William-Crouch and
Dora William-Crouch.
Their Children:
Lonnie J. William-Crouch married. **Their Child:**
Jeremiah Crouch.
Dora William-Crouch, **Her Child:**

Calvin L. William-Hill, His Children: Nickya Martin, Keyana
Danea Martin, Jaiden Lewis Martin, Armani Amir Martin, Kamilah
Blackman and Shakya Martin.
Their Children:
Kamilah Blackman, Her Children: Kamani Blackman, Kah'mir
Spence, Kah'maad Spence, Kasiyah Blackman and Kasi Blackman.
Shakya Martin, Her Child: Shalon Michelle Ricks-Martin.

Martha L. Durham-Fitzpatrick (Aunt MaLue), married
Robert Fitzpatrick Sr.
Their Children: Annie M. Fitzpatrick-Thomas,
Geraldine Fitzpatrick-Thomas, Mary Jane Fitzpatrick-Blash (Sister),
Katie M. Fitzpatrick, Louise Fitzpatrick-Butler,
Robert Fitzpatrick Jr. (Foot), Josephine Fitzpatrick-Coley (Juite)
and Mary A. Fitzpatrick-Thomas.
Their Children:

Louise Fitzpatrick-Butler, married Willie C. Butler Sr., **Their
Children:** Willie C. Butler, Jr. (Boot) and Stan Tavio Butler.
Their Children:
Willie C. Butler Jr. (Boot), His children: Keyandra Butler,
Diamond Butler, Willie C. Butler III (Christain), Zion Butler,
Niaya Butler.
Keyandra Butler: Her children: Arkeyla Butler, Rayven Butler
Stan Tavio Butler: His children: Kateria Butler, Darius Butler
and Tayler Butler
Fernandez Glover-Butler: His children: Kamurie Butler,
Tkhy'a Butler

Mary A. Fitzpatrick-Thomas, married George Thomas Sr. (Sonny). **Their Children:** George Thomas Jr., Ann Marie Thomas (Ree), Tina Thomas, Lillie Mae Thomas (Pluck), Patricia Fitzpatrick-Thomas.
Their Children:
George Thomas Jr., His children: Corey Fitzpatrick-Ellis, Casey Fitzpatrick-Ellis, Cambry Fitzpatrick-Ellis, Caley Fitzpatrick-Ellis, Christopher Fitzpatrick-Denson, Joshua Fitzpatrick-Denson and Nicholas Fitzpatrick-Kemp.
Their children:
Casey Fitzpatrick-Ellis, **His Child:** Kaison Ellis
Christopher D. Fitzpatrick-Denson, **His Children**: Chris'tavione Fitzpatrick-Beauford, Emari C. Fitzpatrick-Beauford, Emija Fitzpatrick-Denson, Jaiden Fitzpatrick-Benjamin, J'Maurion Fitzpatrick-Benjamin, Christopher J. Fitzpatrick-Denson, (2020 Child) and Christopher D. Fitzpatrick-Denson Jr

Ann Marie Thomas (Ree), Her children: Sharieka Fitzpatrick-Thomas and Jamesha Fitzpatrick-Williams.
Their children:
Sharieka Fitzpatrick-Thomas, **Her Children:** Rick Fitzpatrick-Miles and Xyrin Fitzpatrick-Simeton.

Tina Thomas-Washington, married Eric Washington.
Their children: Tracreyone Fitzpatrick-Thomas, Amelia Fitzpatrick-Washington Tamera Fitzpatrick-Washington.
Their Children:
Tracreyone Fitzpatrick-Thomas-**His Child:** Trenton Thomas.

Lillie Mae Thomas (Pluck),
Her children: LaShondra Fitzpatrick-Thomas (Shonamay), Jamarcus Fitzpatrick-Jones and Jalen Fitzpatrick-Thomas.
Their Children:

LaShondra Fitzpatrick-Thomas,
Her Children:
Jamarcus Fitzpatrick-Jones, **His Child:**
Skylar Fitzpatrick-Jones.
Jalen Fitzpatrick-Thomas, **His Children:**
Aaliyah Fitzpatrick-Thomas, and Noah Fitzpatrick-Thomas.

Patricia Fitzpatrick-Thomas, Her children: Shanieki Fitzpatrick, Stephanie Fitzpatrick, Jonathan Fitzpatrick, Patia Fitzpatrick.
Their Children:
Shanieki Fitzpatrick-Rouse, married Antonio Rouse (Boot ball).
Their Children: Zorriah Fitzpatrick-Rouse, Asanti Fitzpatrick-Rouse.
Stephanie Fitzpatrick-Tyler, married Adrian Tyler.
Their Children: Karson Fitzpatrick-Tyler, Kimorra Fitzpatrick-Sanders Kaydynce Fitzpatrick
Jonathan Fitzpatrick-Thomas, His Children: Jayce Fitzpatrick, Tristan Fitzpatrick and Adrain Fitzpatrick.

Geraldine Fitzpatrick-Robinson-Thomas, married Hembree Thomas, died (2016)
Their Children: Sandra Fitzpatrick Robinson (Sloop), Frederick Robinson (died) 1967 and Antonio Robinson (Tony).
Their Children:
Sandra Fitzpatrick-Hollingsworth married Gary Hollingworth Sr. (died)1993:
Their Children:
Javoris V. Hollingsworth, Gary S. Hollingworth Jr., and Lachandria Bond (Chan).
Antonio Robinson married Karla Robinson. **Their Child:** Jamika Robinson
Their Children:
Javoris V. Hollingsworth married Arlene Hollingsworth.
Their children:
Graceyn N. Hollingsworth, Celine Hollingsworth, Elliott Hollingsworth.
LaChandra Fitzpatrick-Bond, Her Child: Zyron Girtman.
Jamika Robinson, Her Child: Raiden Bailey

Mary Jane Fitzpatrick-Carswell-Blash married, Otha Carswell (Butterball) (Died 1989), Blash (Died 2000)
Their Children: Cynthia D. Fitzpatrick-Carswell-Burns married Bobby Burns **Their Children:** Rafael Fitzpatrick-Carswell, Brinequa A.Fitzpatrick-Bloodworth
Rafael Fitzpatrick-Carswell, married Alexis Carswell.
Their children: Riley Carswell, Teyton Carswell and Remeo Carswell.

Katie M. Fitzpatrick, never married/No children. She is the Angel of the Family.

Robert Fitzpatrick Jr. (Foot), married Rose M. Rouse-Fitzpatrick died (2019)
Their Children: Cliff Rouse, Vesha Fitzpatrick.

Josephine Fitzpatrick-Carswell-Coley (Juite), married Aaron Coley.
Her Children: LaShon Carswell-McClinton (Shon)
and Britney Carswell-Garner.
Their Children:
LaShon Carswell-McClinton (Shon) died (2020), Her Child:
Shongarria McClinton
Britney Carswell-Garner, married Reggie Garner Jr.
Their Children: Reggie Carswell-Garner III,
Christian Carswell-Sapp
Annie M. Fitzpatrick-Thomas married Milton Thomas.
Their Child:
Audrey Fitzpatrick-Hart-Welch, Their Children: Jakedrick Fitzpatrick, Maya Fitzpatrick-Hart, and Jasmine Fitzpatrick-Hart-Jackson.
Jakedrick Fitzpatrick, His Children: Jameria Fitzpatrick, Christy Fitzpatrick
Jasmine Fitzpatrick-Hart-Jackson, Her Child: Zoria Jackson
Maya Fitzpatrick-Hart, Her children: Jasmeria Hart, Paris Sinclair and Jayteon Sinclair.

Bobby Link Durham Sr. (Uncle Link) (Died)
married Christine R. Durham (Ain't Pig)
Their Children: Rosa Durham, Kathleen Burden, Annie Burney,
Bobby L. Durham Jr., Ronald Durham and Donald Durham **(twins)**.
Their Children:

Rosa Durham—Her child: Tabitha Durham-Rouse.
Tabitha Durham-Rouse married Kareem Rouse
Their children: Safaree Rouse and Tylik Rouse

Kathleen Durham-Burden married Willie Burden
Their Children: Derrick Burden (D-Word) (died 2013),
Undray Burden,
(Undray's twin died), Twins, Kowombi Burden and Kilwanbi
Burden (died 1994)
Derrick Burden-(D-Word died 2013)
His children: Amber Burden and Nyda Burden
Her children: Amber Burden, **Her children:** Kynleigh Burden
and Carlie Burden.
Kowombi Burden-(Shawn/Bolot)-
His children:
Undray Burden (Snake) married Demetrice Purnell-Burden.
Their children: Draekwon Burden, De'jai Burden, Jaquandre
Burden, Keondre Burden, Akiriah Burden and Jashunbe
Wilson-Burden.
Da'niyah Rivers, Her child: Olivia Rivers.
Jashunbe Wilson-Burden, His Child: Jashun Wilson-Burden.

Annie M. Durham-Burney, Her Children: Physis Durham-
Tharpe, Kimberly Durham-Davis and Artineus Durham-Stuckey.
Their Children:
Physis Durham-Tharpe, married, **Their Children:** Antonius
Burney, Kimberly Durham-Davis, married, **Their Children:**
Willie Davis, Autumn Davis, Kendrick Davis and Chris Davis.
Artineus Durham-Stuckey, He has 1 daughter.

Bobby L. Durham II. married Uletha Durham
His Children: Tahlia Durham-Gleaton, Katahlia Durham-Gleaton
and Bobby L. Durham III.
Their Children:
Tahlia Durham-Gleaton, Katahlia Durham-Gleaton, **Her Child:**
(2020 baby).

Ronald Durham married Bernita Carswell-Durham
Their Children: Kasashia Durham, Mario Durham
and Martiz Durham.
Kasashia Durham, Her Child: Isaiah Durham

Donald Durham married Jacqueline Freeman-Durham.
Their Children: Shaniqua Durham, Donreckio Durham and
Quintina Durham.

DID YOU KNOW: There are (5) Zefnia Durham's in the family.

DID YOU KNOW: That we have more than (15) Ministers in the Crockett Durham and Jordan Families.

DID YOU KNOW: Martha L. Durham-Fitzpatrick (Aunt MartLue), all of her children are alive in (2020).

DID YOU KNOW: There are (3) Aaron Sampson Crockett's in our family.

DID YOU KNOW: Aunt Cash was (94) when she died (2020) she was the oldest child that lived from the Crockett-Durham family.

DID YOU KNOW: Bobby Link Durham Sr. his wife Christine R. Durham (Ain't Pig) is the only wife to be living from the second generation, yet alive in 2020.

DID YOU KNOW: Pauline Durham-Curtis married Iverson Curtis (Uncle Son). He is the only husband of the second generation to be alive in 2020.

DID YOU KNOW: Calvin and Annie Crocket-Durham, have 2 daughters living in 2020 from the second generation.

DID YOU KNOW: That twins are in the genes of the Durham, Jordan and the Crockett families.

DID YOU KNOW: Zefnia Durham Sr. had a Twin sister who died at birth.

ABOUT THE AUTHOR

Avie L. Durham Ringwood-Wilbur is a Retired Army Veteran of 25 years. She has a devoted husband (William) of over 26 years. They have a beautiful family which consists of 3 sons and several grandchildren. She writes a vast amount about her mother and father along with years of ancestry in this book.

Avie L. Durham Ringwood-Wilbur was born to and raised by her parents Sarah and Zefnia Durham, Sr. Her parents had a total of fourteen (14) children. Avie is the twelfth child and the seventh girl. She has 5 five sisters and 3 three brothers living in 2020.

Avie L. Ringwood-Wilbur is the Chief Executive Officer of A-Wilbur, Inc. (aka) AviesHouse, a non-profit Veteran Assistant Center, where she has spent a large percentage of her time helping Veterans. She retired from the United States Army, after honorably serving twenty-five (25) years from 1983-2008. Since 2008, she saw a need to honor veterans. Avieshouse sponsors 3 events a year to support this cause in which she presents personalized American Flags to Veterans who have served in the military.

Avie is very family oriented, exuberant, supportive and greatly involved in educating family members by communicating with them through a natural support system to the extent possibilities. She possesses extremely effective organizational communication skills, verbally and written. She spent countless days and nights along with masses of energy researching the information required to write this book. She has spoken with numerous family members, visited many libraries and web sites such as Ancestry.com, Newspapers.com and Fold 3 in collecting all data.

Avie is highly recognized inside and outside of her community and brings vital services that are efficient, skilled and compassionate to all. Her outstanding Education Credential consists of: Ordained minister, Certified DAV service officer, CEO–A-Wilbur, Inc. (aka) Avieshouse Veteran Assistant Center, Notary Republican, BA–Healthcare Management, BS–Music–Christian Ministry from Dallas Baptist University, MA–Human Services Counseling/specializing in Health & Wellness and School of Behavioral Sciences. Avie is studying Post Graduate Philosophy in Communication at her Alumni, Liberty University, the Flames.

Avie is a fun, loving and caring person who really loves bringing families together. She believes that all families should know about the root of their ancestors. This is what Avie shares in this book.

"Making your mark on the world is hard.
If it were easy everybody would do it.
But it's not.
It takes commitment, and it comes with plenty of failure
along the way.
The real test is not whether you won't it
It 's whether you let it harden or shame you into inaction,
or whether you choose to persevere".
President Obama.

REFERENCES

Clay, Regina (2020). *Foreword: Durham, Crockett and Jordan Documentary*. Williamsburg, Va

Durham III, Zefnia (2000). *Grandchildren's Poem "We All had A Place In Her Heart"*. Gainesville, Florida.

Ringwood-Wilbur, Avie Durham. (2020). *The Jordan-Durham-Crockett Documentary*. Stockbridge, Ga: Salem Author Center, Inc.

Thomas, G. E. (2008). *Yes we can: a biography of President Barack Obama*. New York: Feiwel and Friends.

http://www.open Bible.org

CPSIA information can be obtained
at www.ICGtesting.com
Printed in the USA
LVHW070807050321
680086LV00047B/285